Saturn

Uranus

Neptune

Telescopes and Space Probes

Editor in chief: Paul A. Kobasa
Supplementary Publications: Jeff De La Rosa, Lisa Kwon,
    Christine Sullivan, Scott Thomas, Marty Zwikel
Research: Mike Barr, Cheryl Graham, Jacqueline Jasek,
    Barbara Lightner, Andy Roberts, Loranne Shields
Graphics and Design: Kathy Creech, Sandra Dyrlund,
    Charlene Epple, Tom Evans, Brenda Tropinski
Permissions: Janet Peterson
Indexing: David Pofelski
Pre-Press and Manufacturing: Carma Fazio, Anne Fritzinger,
    Steven Hueppchen, Tina Ramirez
Writer: Kathleen Kain

First edition published 2006. Second edition published 2007.

WORLD BOOK and the GLOBE DEVICE are registered
trademarks or trademarks of World Book, Inc.

World Book, Inc.
233 N. Michigan Avenue
Chicago, IL 60601
U.S.A.

Library of Congress Cataloging-in-Publication Data
Telescopes and space probes. -- 2nd ed.
    p. cm. -- (World Book's solar system & space exploration
library)
    Summary: "Introduction to telescopes and space probes for
primary and intermediate grade students. Includes fun facts,
glossary, resource list and index"--Provided by publisher.
    Includes bibliographical references and index.
    ISBN-13: 978-0-7166-9520-2
    ISBN-10: 0-7166-9520-0
    1. Telescopes--Juvenile literature. 2. Space probes--Juvenile
literature. 3. Outer space--Exploration--Juvenile literature.
QB88.T337 2007
522'.2--dc22
                                    2006030046

ISBN-13 (set): 978-0-7166-9511-0
ISBN-10 (set): 0-7166-9511-1

Printed in the United States of America

1 2 3 4 5 6 7 8 09 08 07 06

**For information about other World Book publications,
visit our Web site at http://www.worldbook.com
or call 1-800-WORLDBK (967-5325).**

**For information about sales to schools and libraries,
call 1-800-975-3250 (United States);
1-800-837-5365 (Canada).**

Picture Acknowledgments: Front Cover: NASA/JPL; Back Cover: © Shigemi Numazawa, Atlas Photo
Bank/Photo Researchers; SOHO, NASA/ESA/HEIC/STScI/AURA, Isaac Newton Group of Telescopes;
Inside Back Cover: © John Gleason, Celestial Images.

SCALA/Art Resource 9; ESO 27; Isaac Newton Group of Telescopes 13; NAIC-Arecibo Observatory 17; NASA
41 (bottom), 43 (bottom), 53, 55 (top); NASA/CXC/SAO 1, 25 (top); NASA/ESA/HEIC/STScI/AURA 25 (bottom),
33; NASA/Johns Hopkins University Applied Physics Laboratory/Carnegie Institution of Washington 45;
NASA/JPL 3, 29 (bottom), 31, 35, 37, 41 (top), 47, 55 (bottom), 57, 59; NASA/JPL/ASU 49; NASA/JPL-Caltech
21; NASA/JPL/Texas A&M/Cornell 51; NASA/JPL/UMD 39; © National Astronomical Observatory of Japan. All
rights reserved. 19; SOHO 23; © Julian Baum, Photo Researchers 61; © John R. Foster, Photo Researchers 7;
© Shigemi Numazawa, Atlas Photo Bank/Photo Researchers 43 (top); © Hugh Turvey, Photo Researchers 6;
© J.R. Eyerman, Time Life Pictures/Getty Images 29 (top); © Richard Wainscoat 15.

Illustrations: Inside Front Cover: WORLD BOOK illustration by Steve Karp; WORLD BOOK illustrations 11.

Astronomers use different kinds of photos to learn about objects in space—such as planets. Many photos show
an object's natural color. Other photos use false colors. Some false-color images show types of light the human
eye cannot normally see. Others have colors that were changed to highlight important features. When
appropriate, the captions in this book state whether a photo uses natural or false color.

WORLD BOOK'S

SOLAR SYSTEM & SPACE EXPLORATION LIBRARY

Telescopes and Space Probes

SECOND EDITION

World Book, Inc.

a Scott Fetzer company
Chicago

Contents

TELESCOPES

If a word is printed in **bold letters that look like this,** that word's meaning is given in the glossary on page 63.

SPACE PROBES

What Is a Telescope?

A telescope is a device that magnifies distant objects, or makes them appear nearer and larger. Telescopes make hard-to-see objects easier to see.

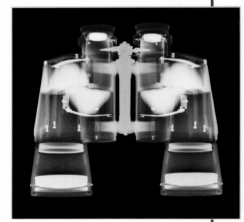

A colored X-ray image of binoculars

Telescopes vary in shape and size. A common telescope looks like a long tube, with one end smaller than the other. **Binoculars** are actually two identical small telescopes joined side by side. Some telescopes are found in large buildings called observatories. Other huge telescopes are carried in **probes** that are sent into space.

Telescopes gather the waves of **electromagnetic energy** that are given off or reflected by distant objects. Optical telescopes (see page 10) gather visible light, the waves of electromagnetic energy the human eye can see. Other kinds of telescopes gather gamma rays or X rays (see page 24), ultraviolet rays (see page 22), infrared waves (see page 18), or radio waves (see page 16).

Looking through
a telescope

Who Invented the Telescope?

In 1608, Dutch eyeglass maker Hans Lippershey (*LIHP urs hy*) placed two glass **lenses** in a narrow tube to make what was probably the first telescope. To make his telescope, Lippershey used a glass lens that was convex— that is, a lens that curves out on both sides—and a concave lens—one that curves in on both sides. When Lippershey looked through his invention at distant objects, the objects appeared larger.

In 1609, Italian **astronomer** Galileo (*GAL uh LAY oh* or *GAL uh LEE oh*) tinkered with Lippershey's telescope design, creating a telescope that made objects appear up to 20 times larger than they looked to the unaided eye. Galileo's telescope also helped him to see things that had never before been seen. For example, in 1610, Galileo discovered four **moons** in **orbit** around Jupiter.

Galileo's telescope, however, produced a haze of color around objects. In 1668, English scientist, astronomer, and mathematician Isaac Newton made a telescope that used a mirror instead of a convex lens, such as Lippershey and Galileo had used. Newton's version of the telescope produced clearer images.

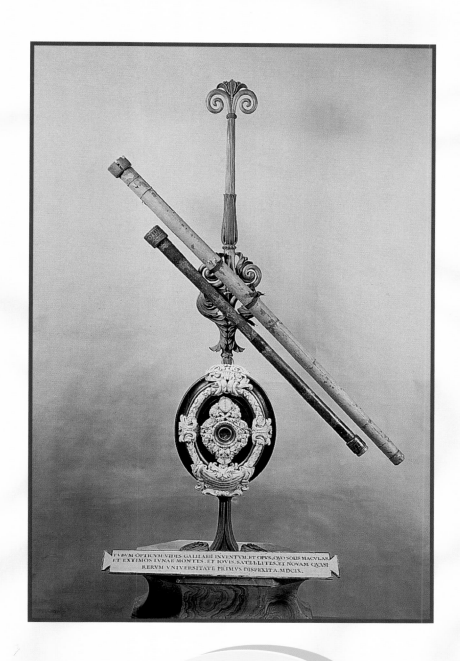

TVBVM OPTICVM VIDES GALILAEII INVENTVM, ET OPVS, QVO SOLIS MACVLAS,
ET EXTIMOS LVNAE MONTES, ET IOVIS SATELLITES, ET NOVAM QVASI
RERVM VNIVERSITATE PRIMVS DISPEXIT A. MDCIX.

Galileo's telescope

What Is an Optical Telescope?

An optical telescope is the most common type of telescope. **Astronomers** use optical telescopes to view such objects as the **moon** and stars. We see objects because light given off or reflected by the objects enters our eye. Optical telescopes work by bending this light.

One kind of optical telescope has a **lens** at its large end. This lens is called the objective lens. It bends the light from the object in a way that forms an image—a picture of the object—inside the telescope. The light from this image goes through another lens, called the eyepiece, at the small end of the telescope. The eyepiece bends this light again and makes the object look big. This bending of light is called refracting, so telescopes with such lenses are called refracting telescopes.

Another kind of optical telescope uses a bowl-shaped mirror instead of lenses. A mirror is said to reflect light, so these telescopes are reflecting telescopes.

Lippershey, Galileo, and Newton (see page 8) all built optical telescopes. Lippershey and Galileo made refracting telescopes, while Newton made a reflecting telescope.

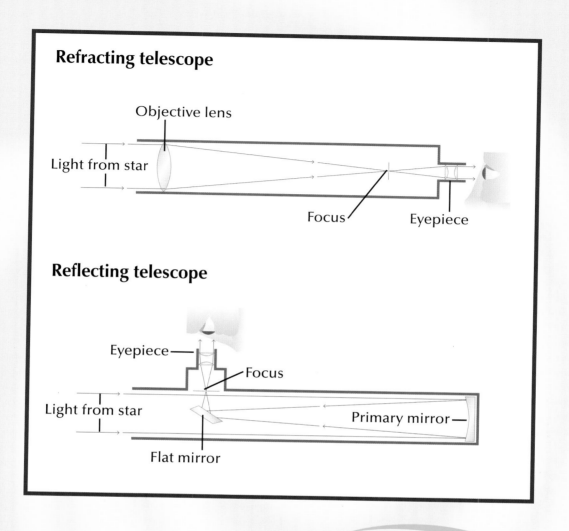

Refracting telescope

Objective lens

Light from star

Focus

Eyepiece

Reflecting telescope

Eyepiece

Focus

Light from star

Primary mirror

Flat mirror

Diagrams of a refracting telescope and a reflecting telescope

How Do Optical Telescopes Make the Invisible Visible?

Before 1609, people thought the surface of the **moon** was smooth. Then Galileo aimed his optical telescope skyward and saw mountains on the moon.

Like the mountains on the moon, many distant objects are invisible to the unaided eye. **Resolution** is a telescope's ability to make distant objects more visible. A high-resolution telescope produces distinct images of objects that blur together when viewed with eyes alone. For example, the brightest star in the sky may turn out to be two stars when observed through even a small telescope.

Astronomers' large telescopes have many times the resolution that smaller telescopes do. One reason is because large telescopes have huge mirrors. These mirrors collect more light than the smaller mirrors on a small telescope.

Telescope size is not the only thing that affects a telescope's resolution. Earth's **atmosphere** can also affect the resolution of ground-based telescopes. Water vapor, air pollution, and even the air itself can blur light from space, reducing a telescope's resolution.

Dome of the William Herschel Telescope on the Canary Islands

Where Are the Largest Optical Telescopes on Earth?

Some of the largest optical telescopes on Earth sit atop Mauna Kea *(MOW nuh KAY uh)*, an inactive volcano located on the island of Hawaii.

The volcano climbs from its base on the floor of the Pacific Ocean to its peak at 13,796 feet (4,205 meters) above sea level. The top of Mauna Kea towers high above Hawaii's clouds and smog. The telescopes atop Mauna Kea have very high **resolution** because the light they gather passes through less of Earth's **atmosphere.** The dry, clear air at the top of the volcano also increases resolution.

The site at Mauna Kea includes 13 major telescopes. The biggest of these are called Keck I and Keck II. Both are optical-reflector telescopes. But, instead of having one large mirror, like reflectors usually have, each of these telescopes has 36 six-sided mirrors mounted together. The combined surface of the mirrors measures 33 feet (10 meters) across.

The observatories on
Mauna Kea, Hawaii

What Is a Radio Telescope?

A radio telescope collects the faint radio waves that come from objects in space. Radio waves are an invisible form of **electromagnetic energy.** You cannot see radio waves, but radio waves we generate on Earth are used to transmit music to your radio. Using a radio telescope, **astronomers** can detect the radio waves that stars give off.

These telescopes work by capturing radio waves in a large, bowl-shaped piece of equipment that is called a dish antenna, or simply a dish. This dish reflects radio waves the same way a mirror reflects light waves. But radio waves are much longer than light waves, so a radio telescope's dish has to be much larger than the mirror of an optical telescope. The dish on the world's largest radio telescope, located at the Arecibo Observatory in Puerto Rico, measures 1,000 feet (305 meters) across. This is more than 30 times the size of the mirrors on the Keck telescopes (see page 14).

The dish of a radio telescope sends the radio waves to another part of the telescope, and in that area the waves are changed into electric signals. A radio receiver strengthens the signals. It also keeps track of the point in space that the signals came from, for instance, the star being observed.

The radio telescope at
Arecibo, Puerto Rico

What Is an Infrared Telescope?

An infrared telescope creates images from infrared waves. These are a type of **electromagnetic energy** that resembles visible light, but which cannot be seen by the human eye. Warm objects give off infrared rays.

Most infrared telescopes are reflectors. They use a bowl-shaped mirror to collect infrared rays. Cool stars and stars in the process of forming show up well in infrared images.

To produce true images, infrared telescopes need special treatment. Heat from the telescope can interfere with images of objects in space. So an infrared telescope must be kept a few degrees above absolute zero, which is -459.67 °F (-273.15 °C). Also, this type of telescope must be placed high up where the air is thin and dry, because gases in the **atmosphere** block infrared rays.

Some telescopes, such as the Infrared Telescope Facility of the National Aeronautics and Space Administration (NASA), are designed to make observations only in infrared light. Other telescopes, such as the Subaru (see facing page), can observe in both visible and infrared light.

Japan's Subaru Telescope (below) and an infrared image of a young star taken with that telescope

Why Would an Infrared Telescope Tag Along After Earth?

Earth's **atmosphere** blocks many infrared rays. But sending an infrared telescope into **orbit** poses a problem. An orbiting telescope can carry only so much coolant. Coolant is a substance that prevents the telescope from becoming too warm. If the telescope gets too warm, the warmth interferes with the infrared rays. When the coolant runs out, the telescope can no longer make infrared images.

In August 2003, NASA launched an infrared telescope called the Spitzer Space Telescope. To help keep it cool, Spitzer carries a solar shield. This shield protects the telescope from the heat of the sun. Also, Spitzer has a unique orbit. Instead of orbiting Earth, Spitzer trails behind Earth as the **planet** travels its orbit around the sun. Spitzer's orbit allows the telescope to stay far enough away from Earth to protect it from the planet's infrared **radiation.** Trailing Earth allows Spitzer's temperature to remain around -450 °F (-270 °C) without the use of a lot of coolant.

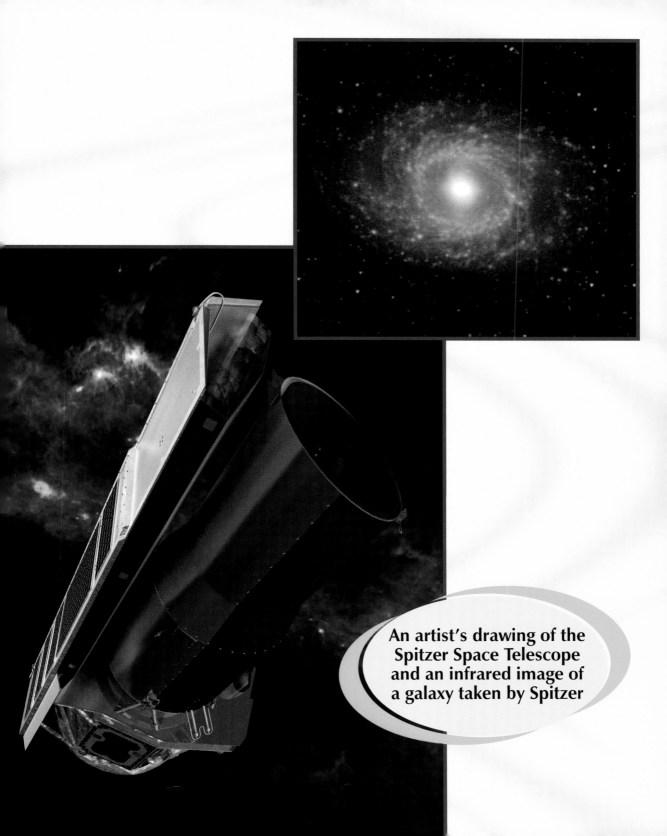

An artist's drawing of the Spitzer Space Telescope and an infrared image of a galaxy taken by Spitzer

What Is an Ultraviolet Telescope?

An ultraviolet telescope is one used to study ultraviolet waves. Ultraviolet is a form of **electromagnetic energy.** Hot objects give off these kinds of waves. The sun is the major source of ultraviolet rays in our **solar system,** but newly formed stars give off much more ultraviolet energy than the sun does. Scientists use ultraviolet waves to study such objects as these stars, the sun, and **quasars.** Ultraviolet telescopes are also used to study how stars form. These kinds of telescopes are placed on space **probes** and launched into space.

To study the shortest ultraviolet wavelengths, which are called extreme ultraviolet wavelengths (EUV), **astronomers** turn to such telescopes as the Solar and Heliospheric Observatory (SOHO). SOHO is a joint project of NASA and the European Space Agency (ESA). Launched in 1995, SOHO observes ultraviolet light from the star at the center of our solar system, the sun. The SOHO telescopes have special mirrors shaped like tubes. The EUV rays reflect off the insides of the tubes and onto a point called the **focus.**

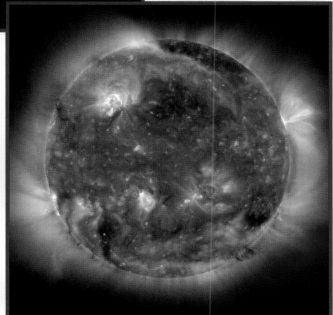

An artist's drawing of SOHO and an ultraviolet image of the sun taken by SOHO

What Are X-ray and Gamma-ray Telescopes?

X-ray and gamma-ray telescopes are used to examine the hottest spots in space.

X rays are a type of **electromagnetic energy** that have even shorter wavelengths on the electromagnetic **spectrum** than does ultraviolet light. Because the **atmosphere** absorbs (takes in) such short wavelengths as X rays and gamma rays, telescopes used to study these wavelengths are launched into space.

The newest X-ray telescopes have mirrors like the ones in some extreme ultraviolet (EUV) telescopes (see page 22). These mirrors are shaped like tubes. The rays reflect off the inside of the tubes. NASA's Chandra X-ray Observatory, launched in 1999, is the most advanced X-ray telescope and produces the most detailed images.

The shortest wavelengths of all are gamma rays. Gamma-ray telescopes track down the high-energy bursts that emit gamma rays. Scientists think that **supernovae** or the collapse of a massive star into a **black hole** may be responsible for some gamma-ray bursts.

An artist's drawing of Chandra and an X-ray image of Saturn's rings taken by Chandra

What Is an Observatory?

An observatory is a place where **astronomers** study **planets,** stars, **galaxies,** and other objects in space. What an observatory looks like and where it is located depends upon what astronomers are studying.

Visible light from stars, for instance, will pass through Earth's **atmosphere.** So, optical telescopes used to study objects that give off visible light can be placed on Earth's surface. The telescopes in these observatories are housed in small buildings that are often dome-shaped. Because the atmosphere blurs light waves, these observatories are often built on mountaintops to reduce this blurring.

Radio waves also pass through the atmosphere, so observatories that house radio telescopes can be based on Earth. Such telescopes, however, must be shielded from the radio waves that are used by people for broadcast purposes, so radio observatories are often built in remote areas. Radio observatories can be one large dish or a large number of dishes grouped together.

Earth's atmosphere blocks such **electromagnetic energy as** gamma rays, X rays, and some wavelengths of infrared and ultraviolet rays. Therefore, observatories that observe these wavelengths are sometimes based in space aboard **satellites.**

Enclosures housing telescopes at the European Southern Observatory in Chile, and an infrared image of Uranus taken at that observatory

Uranus surrounded by its rings and some of its moons

What Is the Largest Telescope in Orbit?

In April 1990, the space shuttle Discovery launched the Hubble Space Telescope. The Hubble, named for American **astronomer** Edwin P. Hubble (1889-1953), is the largest telescope in **orbit.** It circles the Earth about 380 miles (610 kilometers) above the **atmosphere.**

The Hubble is a reflecting telescope, so it observes visible light. It can also observe ultraviolet and infrared light. This light is blocked by Earth's atmosphere, but the Hubble gets a clear view of things in space because it travels above the air that surrounds Earth. Although air seems clear, it makes stars and other objects in space look blurry. For example, stars seem to twinkle because their light comes to our eyes through moving layers of air. So, while telescopes on Earth may get a blurry image, the Hubble often gets a sharp picture.

Although the Hubble operates in space, it is controlled from the ground. Astronomers at NASA use radio commands to tell the telescope where to point. Then instruments aboard the telescope take pictures and record data, or information.

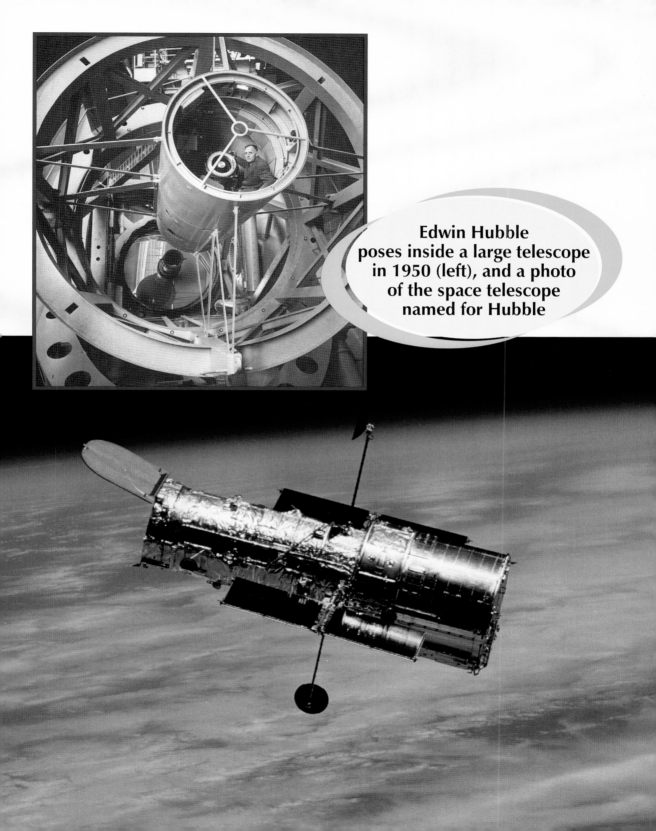

Edwin Hubble poses inside a large telescope in 1950 (left), and a photo of the space telescope named for Hubble

How Does Hubble Stay in Orbit?

Imagine a tetherball. If you lift the ball away from the pole and then release it, the ball will swing back down and hit the pole. But, if instead of just letting go of the ball you give it a push to one side, as the ball swings back it will miss the pole on that side. On the ball's return, it will miss the pole on the other side. As it misses the pole each time, the ball travels around the pole in essentially a circle. The string is constantly pulling the ball toward the pole, but the ball's **momentum** carries it around the pole, preventing a collision.

Imagine that the ball is the Hubble Space Telescope, the pole is Earth, and the string is **gravity.** The telescope constantly falls toward Earth because of Earth's gravity. But, because of the telescope's momentum, it misses Earth. This causes the telescope to travel around the **planet** in a roughly circular **orbit.** The momentum was given to the telescope during its initial release by the space shuttle. The Hubble slowly gets lower (closer to Earth) in its orbit as the telescope loses some momentum. But when space shuttle astronauts have visited the telescope, they have pushed it into a higher orbit again.

Space shuttle astronauts make repairs to the Hubble as it orbits Earth

Why Is Hubble So Important?

Hubble is important because it launched a new age of astronomy. The telescope's images show distant **nebulae,** colliding **galaxies,** and evidence of **black holes.** Its images also record the birth and death of stars and take us to the edge of the visible **universe.**

Light from distant stars travels millions and sometimes billions of years before it reaches us. So, Hubble's pictures of stars and galaxies actually record the stars' past, not their present. These records give us clues to how our galaxy, the Milky Way, began and how it might end. When we see an old star die, for instance, we learn what is in store in the far distant future for our own star, the sun.

Other Hubble images come from our own **solar system.** For example, in 1994, pieces of an exploded **comet** crashed into Jupiter. The largest pieces probably measured a few miles (kilometers) across. Most pieces struck with a tremendous force. The impacts shot gas thousands of miles (kilometers) into space. As the drama unfolded, Hubble captured the highlights.

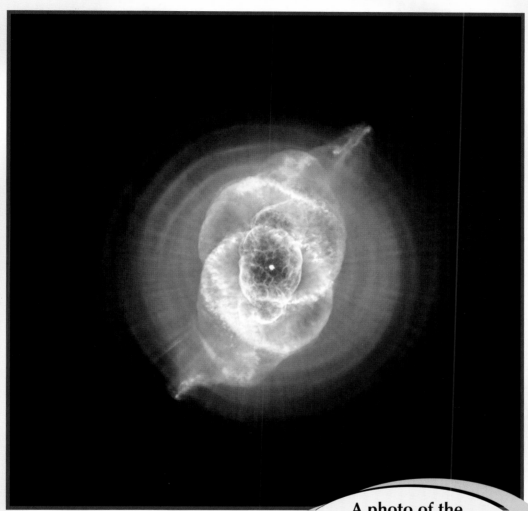

A photo of the
Cat's Eye Nebula, taken
in natural-color by the
Hubble Space Telescope

What Is a Space Probe?

A space **probe** is an unpiloted rocket shot into space in order to carry out a mission. Usually, the mission is to gather data (information), which the probe then radios back to Earth. Occasionally, a probe will gather samples of material from a distant object or from space itself. Such a probe may return the samples to Earth, or it may analyze (determine the nature of) the samples and radio back the results.

Some probes journey to the far corners of space and never return. Others travel in an **orbit** around the sun or around a **planet.**

Still other probes land on planets and **moons.** Scientists classify this kind of probe according to the way it lands. A probe that lands without slowing down is called an impact vehicle, or impactor. Another type of probe, a lander, performs experiments and records data after coming to rest on the planet's or moon's surface. A special kind of lander, called a **rover,** can move around after landing and explore the surface of a planet or moon.

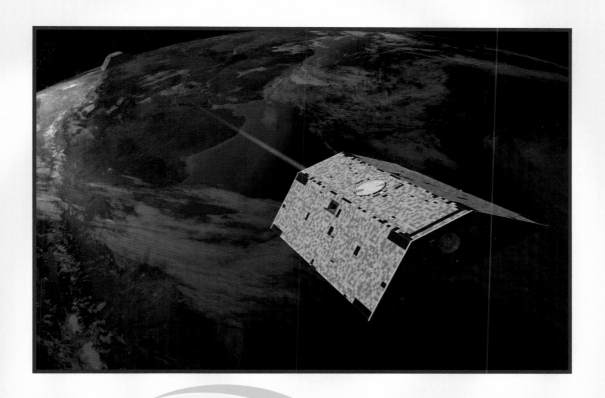

An artist's drawing of
twin space probes used
in NASA's Gravity
Recovery and Climate
Experiment (GRACE)

What Kinds of Information Do Space Probes Collect?

Probes collect information about various conditions in space. For example, they measure the temperature of **comets, moons, planets,** and stars. Then they radio their data back to Earth.

Probes may also conduct experiments. Some probes take samples of gases and other materials from Earth and record how the materials react to conditions in space. Other probes dig up soil samples on a moon or a planet and analyze (determine the nature of) these samples.

Probes can be used to determine what types and levels of **radiation** exist in certain areas. Probes can also be used to observe and report on objects near the probe's target object. For example, a probe sent to a specific planet might also be used to study that planet's rings and moons.

Probes also take photographs of distant objects like planets and moons. These stunning photos often give the first real idea of what an object looks like.

An artist's drawing of NASA's Mars Reconnaissance Orbiter

Why Are Probes Sent Instead of People?

   Probes are very useful to scientists. They are safer than piloted missions and they can be used to study places that humans could never go to and survive. For example, NASA recently used probes on a mission called Deep Impact to study a **comet.**

   This mission used two probes. One was an impactor—a kind of probe that strikes the target object without slowing down—that measured about 3 by 3 feet (0.9 by 0.9 meter). The other probe was a larger, **fly-by** craft not meant to land on the surface of the comet being studied.

   In January 2005, the Deep Impact spacecraft was launched to a comet known as Comet Tempel 1. On July 4, 2005, the impactor probe hit the comet and created a large **crater.** The impactor took pictures of the comet before smashing into it, and the larger fly-by probe took pictures of the destruction as it happened. The data sent from the probe helped scientists to determine what the comet was made of. Scientists hope the data will help determine some details about the origins of our **solar system.**

An artist's concept of the collision of NASA's Deep Impact with a comet

What Was the "Space Race"?

An object in space that revolves around a planet is a **satellite.** In July 1955, the United States announced its plan to launch the first artificial satellite. Soon after, the Soviet Union—a large European nation that existed from the 1920's through the 1990's—declared that it too planned to launch a human-made satellite into space. The "space race" was on!

On October 4, 1957, the Soviets launched Sputnik (*SPUHT nihk*)—later called Sputnik 1—and beat the Americans at entering space. Sputnik circled Earth every 96 minutes for 3 months. As it did, it radioed a steady "beep-beep" back to Earth. In November, the Soviets sent up Sputnik 2. American scientists tried to catch up. They launched their satellite on December 6, 1957. But after seconds in the air, the satellite crashed to the ground.

On January 31, 1958, Americans put Explorer 1 into **orbit.** Later that year, Congress passed the National Aeronautics and Space Act, which created NASA. Today, NASA and Russian scientists (former Soviets) no longer compete. They often work together on such projects as the International Space Station.

A poster produced by the Jet Propulsion Laboratory, which built Explorer 1

EXPLORER 1

AMERICA'S FIRST EARTH SATELLITE

jpl

JET PROPULSION LABORATORY

CALIFORNIA INSTITUTE OF TECHNOLOGY

Where Did Early Space Probes Go?

The favorite destination for early space **probes** was the **moon.** The first probe to come close to the moon was Luna 1, launched by the Soviet Union. (*Luna* is Latin for "moon.") In January 1959, Luna 1 passed within about 3,700 miles (6,000 kilometers) of the moon. On March 4, 1959, NASA's Pioneer 4 flew by the moon but was too far away to get detailed pictures of it.

Six months later, the Soviets' Luna 2 became the first probe to hit the moon. The impact released small Russian medals onto the moon's surface. In October, Luna 3 traveled around the moon and photographed the far side of the moon, which is the half of the moon that is always turned away from Earth.

The moon remained a common target throughout the 1960's. The Soviets launched a hard-lander craft called Luna 9 in 1966. NASA responded with a series of soft-landers named Surveyor. Surveyor 1 sent more than 11,000 images of the moon's surface back to Earth.

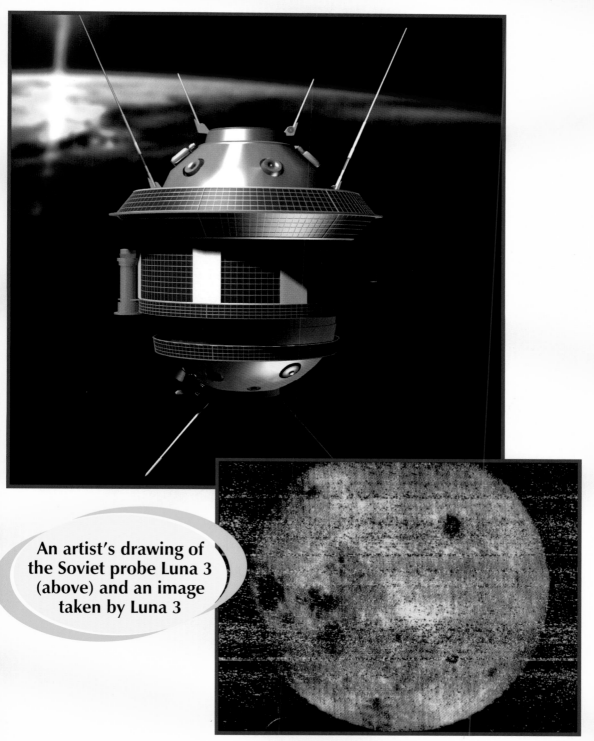

An artist's drawing of the Soviet probe Luna 3 (above) and an image taken by Luna 3

Image of the far side of the moon, taken by Luna 3 on October 7, 1959

When Did Space Probes Reach Venus, Mercury, and Mars?

Americans launched successful **fly-bys** past Venus in 1962, 1967, and 1974. Yet the first **probe** to actually land on Venus was the Soviet Union's Venera 7. It touched down in 1970.

NASA's Mariner 10 flew by Mercury in 1974 and took pictures of the planet's moonlike surface. In 2004, NASA launched Messenger, a probe scheduled to start orbiting Mercury in 2011. Neither the United States nor Russia has landed a probe on Mercury.

Traffic to Mars has become increasingly heavy since the 1970's. In 1971, the Soviet Mars 2 lander crashed to the surface. Days later, Mars 3 completed the first successful soft landing on Mars. The probe transmitted for 20 seconds and then contact was lost. Following close behind, NASA's Mariner 9 went into orbit around Mars and took numerous images of the **planet.** The busiest probes on Mars in the 1970's were NASA's Viking 1 and Viking 2. Both probes arrived in 1976 and took pictures and issued weather reports for several years.

An artist's concept of NASA's Messenger probe orbiting Mercury

How Did Pathfinder Collect Facts About Mars?

NASA's Pathfinder **probe** spent seven months flying to Mars. Then it landed on July 4, 1997. Inside, the probe carried a six-wheeled **rover** called Sojourner. The rover was about the size of a toy wagon.

Sojourner rolled out of the probe on July 6 and started to analyze the Martian soil and rocks. Then the vehicle passed its data (information) to Pathfinder. Pathfinder, in turn, radioed the data to NASA scientists on Earth. Sojourner and Pathfinder kept the information flowing for almost three months.

During those months, Sojourner traveled a little over 100 yards (91 meters). Scientists on Earth steered Sojourner with radio signals. For example, they radioed the vehicle when they wanted it to turn left and when they wanted it to back up. But the signals took about 10 minutes to travel from Earth to Mars. As a result, scientists could not help Sojourner avoid obstacles in its path. Instead, Sojourner used special sensors it had on board to go around **craters** and boulders.

An artist's concept of NASA's Sojourner (above) and a natural-color image of Mars

What Other Probes Have Studied Mars?

In 1996, NASA launched a **probe** called the Mars Global Surveyor. Its main job was to map the surface of Mars. In addition, the orbiting probe's camera took remarkable pictures that suggested water may once have existed on Mars.

In 2001, NASA launched the Mars Odyssey. In 2002, this probe discovered more than enough ice on Mars to fill Lake Michigan twice. Most of the ice lay just below the surface near the Martian south pole. Some photos taken by Mars Odyssey showed channels on the planet's surface that provided further evidence that water may have once flowed on Mars.

In 2003, the European Space Agency (ESA) launched a probe called Mars Express, which sent pictures of the Martian surface showing an icecap covering the planet's southernmost region. NASA's Mars Reconnaissance Orbiter launched in 2005 and began orbiting Mars in 2006. Its mission was to study the distribution (the area over which a thing is spread) of water on Mars.

This channel gives evidence of waterflow on Mars

Mars Odyssey black-and-white photos

Clouds on Mars

What Are Spirit and Opportunity?

Spirit and Opportunity are **rovers**—vehicles that rove around searching for information. NASA put them on Mars in January 2004. Spirit landed in an area of Mars known as the Gusev **Crater.** Opportunity landed in an area known as the Meridiani Planum. The rovers were sent to Mars to analyze soil and rocks. Opportunity discovered sulfate salts in the rock. On Earth, sulfate salts occur only in rocks formed in or exposed to water. NASA scientists concluded that liquid water may once have covered the Meridiani Planum.

The rovers' mission was to last only three Earth months, but it has lasted much longer. Spirit and Opportunity were still on the job in January 2005, when Opportunity ran across a rare **meteorite** *(MEE tee uh ryt)* made of **iron.** It was the first meteorite found on any **planet** other than Earth.

In November 2005, Spirit passed an important milestone, having explored the planet's surface for a full Martian year (nearly 2 Earth years). Opportunity completed a full Martian year in December 2005.

A Martian sunset captured by Spirit in a natural-color photomosaic

Why Were Plaques Aboard the Probes that Studied Jupiter?

The first **probe** to go near Jupiter was NASA's Pioneer 10 in 1973. In this case, "near" meant within 81,000 miles (130,000 kilometers) of Jupiter's cloud cover. Pioneer 11 followed in 1974. After its Jupiter **fly-by,** Pioneer 11 headed for Saturn.

After completing their missions, the probes sped out of the **solar system.** NASA scientists had considered the possibility that somewhere in the **universe,** alien beings—sometimes called extraterrestrials—might find the probes one day. So, aboard the Pioneer 10 and 11 spacecraft, scientists put plaques with a picture message that they hoped beings from any planet would be able to understand. The plaques were designed by a famous American **astronomer,** Carl Sagan (1934-1996). The picture on the plaques shows a man and a woman, a diagram of our solar system, the position of the sun within the Milky Way Galaxy, and other symbols relating to scientific knowledge.

A plaque, bearing a message about Earth, attached to the Pioneer space probe

What Did the Voyager and Galileo Probes Discover?

NASA launched Voyager 1 and Voyager 2 in 1977. The **probes** passed by the outer **planets** Jupiter, Saturn, Uranus *(YUR uh nuhs or yu RAY nuhs),* and Neptune and took photos of clouds on Uranus. These probes also photographed faint rings circling Jupiter. And Voyager 2 captured images of a huge storm on Neptune. All together, the Voyagers discovered almost two dozen **moons** in **orbit** around these planets. Voyager pictures from Neptune's moon Triton showed spouts erupting nitrogen. The streams of nitrogen were as high as 5 miles (8 kilometers) above Triton's surface. Voyager also sent pictures showing active volcanoes on Jupiter's moon Io.

In 1989, NASA sent Galileo to Jupiter for a closer look. Galileo was a two-part probe. The larger probe released a small probe into Jupiter's **atmosphere.** After about an hour in the atmosphere's extreme heat, the small probe shut down. Meanwhile, the spacecraft orbited the planet and observed Jupiter's moons. It found that lava from volcanoes on the moon Io was hotter than lava on Earth. It also found evidence that an ocean of water may lie beneath the icy surface of the moon Europa.

NASA workers getting Galileo ready for launch (above) and an image Galileo sent from space

Hot lava can be seen during a volcanic eruption on Io in this false-color photomosaic from Galileo

What Probe Was First to Orbit Saturn?

In 1997, NASA launched a **probe** called Cassini. The spacecraft included a smaller probe called Huygens *(HOY gehns)*, built by the European Space Agency (ESA). Cassini-Huygen's job was to study Saturn, its rings, and its **moons.**

Cassini began **orbiting** Saturn in 2004. On December 25, 2004, Cassini released Huygens. Three weeks later, the small probe parachuted through the smoggy **atmosphere** of Saturn's moon Titan. For 2½ hours, the probe analyzed chemicals, recorded sounds, and measured wind speeds as it floated to the moon's surface. It also shot pictures of what looked like riverbeds on Titan's surface. The probe landed in a pool of dirty ice.

Meanwhile, the Cassini spacecraft observed Saturn's rings. The orbiter's images showed a puzzling gap in the outer ring. Scientists believed that a moon, not yet discovered at that time, caused the gap. In May 2005, Cassini produced images that showed this moon, which measured 4 miles (7 kilometers) across. NASA scientists hope to discover new moons as Cassini continues to orbit Saturn.

An artist's concept of the
Huygens probe landing
on Titan

What Has NASA Learned from Stardust and NEAR?

Scientists think that the gas, ice, rock, and dust in **comets** are left over from the formation of the outer **planets.** Some scientists believe that comets may have brought water and **carbon**—the building blocks of life—to Earth. To test these ideas, NASA and other space agencies have launched space **probes** that target comets. For example, in 2004, NASA's Stardust probe flew by a comet known as Comet Wild 2. Stardust collected samples of the dust and gas surrounding the comet's nucleus, or core. The probe returned to Earth with these samples in January 2006.

Other recent probes have targeted **asteroids.** NASA used the Near Earth Asteroid Rendezvous (NEAR) probe to measure the asteroids Mathilde and Eros. NEAR also studied the makeup of these two asteroids. According to NEAR, Mathilde is about 40 miles (65 kilometers) wide and very light. So, scientists suspect Mathilde's rock is full of holes, like a sponge. Eros is heavier and slightly smaller than Mathilde. Scientists assume that Eros is probably solid rock.

Comet Wild 2 in a natural-color
composite image sent by Stardust

What Is "Space Junk"?

In September 2006, astronauts from NASA's space shuttle Atlantis were adding a new piece to the International Space Station, when two bolts they needed to install a section of the station were lost in space. The astronauts used spare bolts to make the connection, but two more pieces of "space junk" were created.

Since the first launch of a rocket into space, quite a lot of things have accumulated and are still either **orbiting** or hanging around in space. Scientists call this space junk, and such junk includes burned-out rocket boosters, pieces of rocket bodies, and an old glove from a spacesuit.

NASA and the U.S. Air Force track space junk that is longer than 4 inches (10 centimeters). The two bolts lost by the Atlantis crew brought the count of pieces of space junk large enough to be tracked to 9,925. But around 90,000 smaller objects are also orbiting Earth. Scientists are concerned about the space junk that **orbits** Earth because it could damage **satellites,** shuttles, or other important objects in space. Some space junk orbits Earth at speeds of more than 15,000 miles (24,100 kilometers) per hour.

An artist's conception
of space junk

FUN FACTS About TELESCOPES & SPACE PROBES

★ The only two **planets** in our **solar system** that the Hubble Space Telescope has not photographed are Earth and Mercury. Earth is too close to Hubble, and Mercury is too close to the sun. If by chance Hubble aimed at the sun instead of the planet, its instruments (the devices used for measuring, recording, and controlling the telescope) would be damaged.

★ Although people cannot see ultraviolet light without special instruments, bumble bees and some other insects can!

★ Sputnik is Russian for "traveling companion."

★ During the late 1960's, U.S. Lunar Orbiters discovered "bumps" in the gravity field around the **moon.** Without this information, NASA astronauts on the Apollo mission may not have been able to land safely on the moon in 1969.

★ The third nation to send a **probe** to the moon was Japan. The probe went into orbit on March 14, 1990, but controllers lost contact soon after.

★ Nine-year-old third-grader Sofi Collis came up with the names Spirit and Opportunity for the Mars **rovers** launched in 2003. She had entered a "Name the Rovers" contest.

★ Mars Odyssey was named for the science-fiction story "2001: A Space Odyssey" by British author Arthur C. Clarke (1917-).

Glossary

teroid A small body made of rock, carbon, or etal that orbits the sun. Most asteroids are tween the orbits of Mars and Jupiter.

tronomer A scientist who studies stars and anets.

mosphere The mass of gases that surrounds a anet.

noculars A double telescope joined as a unit use with both eyes at once.

ack hole A region of space where gravity is so ong that nothing can escape from it.

rbon A nonmetallic chemical element.

met A small body made of dirt and ice that bits the sun.

ater A bowl-shaped depression on the surface a moon or planet.

ectromagnetic energy Energy formed of waves eated by the back and forth motion (oscillation) electric charges. These waves travel through ace at the speed of light—about 186,282 miles 99,792 kilometers) per second. From longest to ortest, the rays in the electromagnetic spectrum e radio waves, infrared rays, ultraviolet rays, ays, and gamma rays.

-by Flight whereby a spacecraft flies near to an ject in space but does not land on or orbit that ject.

cus The point at which rays of light, heat, or her radiation meet after being reflected from a rror or bent by a lens.

laxy A group of billions of stars forming one tem.

avity The effect of a force of attraction that acts tween all objects because of their mass (that is, e amount of matter the objects have).

n A metallic chemical element.

ns A curved piece of glass, or something like ss, used in such items as telescopes.

eteorite A mass of stone or metal from outer ace that has reached the surface of a planet thout burning up in that planet's atmosphere.

momentum A measure of the motion of an object. The momentum of a moving object equals how much matter the object has multiplied by the object's speed.

moon A smaller body that orbits a planet.

nebula A cloud of dust particles and gases in space.

orbit The path that a smaller body takes around a larger body, for instance, the path that a planet takes around the sun. Also, to travel in an orbit.

planet A large, round body in space that orbits a star. A planet must have sufficient gravitational pull to clear other objects from the area of its orbit.

probe An unpiloted device sent to explore space. Most probes send data (information) from space.

quasar A very bright object in space that gives off powerful blue light and radio waves.

radiation Energy given off in the form of waves or small particles of matter.

resolution A telescope's ability to make distant objects able to be seen more clearly.

rover A vehicle for exploratory travel on the surface of a planet or moon.

satellite An artificial satellite is an object built by people and launched into space, where it continuously orbits Earth or some other body.

solar system A group of bodies in space made up of a star and the planets and other objects orbiting around that star.

spectrum The band of colors formed when a beam of white light is broken up by being passed through a prism or by some other means. Also, the band of colors formed when any other form of radiant energy is broken up. The ends of such a band are not visible to the eye but are studied with special instruments.

supernova An exploding star.

universe Everything that exists anywhere in space and time.

Index

For more information about telescopes and space probes, try these resources:

Adventure in Space: The Flight to Fix the Hubble, by Elaine Scott, Hyperion Books for Children, (Reprint) 1998

Hubble: The Mirror on the Universe, by Robin Kerrod, Firefly Books, 2003

Looking Inside: Telescopes and the Night Sky, by Ron Schultz, John Muir Publishing, 1992

Satellites and Space Probes, by Bobbie Kalman, Crabtree Publishing, 1998

http://hubblesite.org/
http://saturn.jpl.nasa.gov/home/index.cfm
http://voyager.jpl.nasa.gov/
http://www.ing.iac.es/
http://www.worldspaceflight.com/probes/